Sky Land
A Southwestern Cycle

Michael L. Johnson

WOODLEY PRESS

ISBN: 978-0-9817334-8-7
        0-9817334-8-4

WOODLEY PRESS
Washburn University
1700 SW College Avenue
Topeka, Kansas 66621

Edited by Gary Lechliter
Cover photo by Michael L. Johnson
Author photo by Lauren Johnson
Book design by Pam LeRow
Printed by Lightning Source

For Kathleen

Contents

Sky Land: A Preface ix

The Southwesterners 1
Dodge City 2
Boot Hill..4
Southwestern Kansas, 1897..5
Highway 56 6
Panhandle Woman 7
Oklahoma 8
Alexandre Hogue, *Dust Bowl* (1933)..9
Dalhart, Texas 10
Uncle Bill's West Texas Ranch 11
Lone Star...12
Prickly Pear 13
Fear and Loathing in the Grasslands 14
In Eastern New Mexico 15
In October 1541, Coronado Writes to the King
    of Spain about the Llano Estacado 16
Tierra Encantada..17
Sixty in Springer 18
George McJunkin Discovers Folsom Man 19
Jiggs Porter Remembers Ranching during the 1930s...................20
Eagle Nest..21
Taos Pueblo 22
A Photograph of Kit Carson 23
The Art of R. C. Gorman 24
Barbara Sachi's Photograph *Café with Auto with*
    Café with Auto 25
Early Spring in Española..26
White Rock Overlook 27
Los Alamos..28
The Valle Grande Caldera...29
Tsankawi Sky 30
Ansel Adams...31
Abiquiu..32
Georgia O'Keeffe in New Mexico..33
Pueblo Bonito...34
Highway 666 35
William A. Suys Jr., *Abbondanza I*...36
B. B. Dunne..37
At the Pink Adobe..38
Bull-Roarer 39
July Rain in the Sangre de Cristos 40
The Staircase of the Loretto Chapel..41

María Benítez at the Radisson 42
Mourning Doves 43
Santa Fe Dawn 44
October at Rancho Viejo 45
Tecolote 46
Piñon 47
Cabezón Peak 48
Louis Owens at Albuquerque International, July 24, 2002 49
Ben Wittick, *Tzashima and Her Husband, Governor
    of Laguna, Laguna Pueblo, ca. 1885* 50
Ácoma Pueblo 51
Matanza in Belén 52
The Very Large Array 53
Trinity Site 54
Chiaroscuro 55
Hillsboro 56
Roswell 57
The Navajo Point of View 58
Kingston 59
Lunch in Old Mesilla 60
A History of New Mexico in Spanish 61
El Paso/Juárez 62
Santo in an Abandoned House near Lordsburg 63
Poco Tiempo 64
Sonoran Twilight 65
Skeleton Canyon 66
Medicine Man 67
Jeff Kidder (1875-1908) 68
Morgan S. Earp: A Short Short Story 69
Cilantro in Sonoita 70
Cochise County Realtor 71
Tucson 72
The Seri 73
Sabino Canyon in Spring 74
North of Tucson: August 75
Sabino Canyon in Fall 76
Barrio Histórico 77
Edward Abbey's Grave 78
Arizona Borderland 79
Old Route 66 80
Highway 40 81
Las Vegas 82
Margaritas at Lake Mead 83
Nevada 84
The Great Basin 85
John Wesley Powell 86

Grand Canyon 87
A Ponderosa Pine in the Kaibab National Forest 88
Mountain Meadows, 1999...89
Everett Ruess...90
A Veteran Downwinder Talks about Snow Canyon 91
The Southwestern Grid 92
Monument Valley..93
Native Poetry: The Lesson of Canyon de Chelly 94
Mesa Verde..95
Red Mountain Pass 96
A Bad Moment in Colorado..97
Pagosa Springs..98
William H. Jackson Observes the Mount of the Holy
    Cross from the Summit of Notch Mountain 99
The Saga of Mart Duggan 100
Teller House, Central City 101
At William Cody's Grave 102
Country Love: Eastern Colorado 103
Garden of the Gods...104

For Alain Lasfargues: An Epilogue 107

Acknowledgments 109

Sky Land: A Preface

I visited that space,
open to everything,
and strove to know it well.

The spirit of the place
gave me the voice to sing
the tales I have to tell.

The Southwesterners

Craving the fabled wild,
they plundered through its world.
Profligately they killed

bison, bear, Indian.
They ruled by horse and gun,
planted dry soil, hoped rain

would come. They stripped, railed, mined,
gridded, fenced, dammed, drilled land
they dreamed subdued, contained.

Too soon farms turned to dust
bowls, booms busts, towns malls, vast
deserts limbos of waste.

Too late some wished it all
untamed again and whole,
unchanged by greed's white will.

Dodge City

In 1821 William Becknell's packtrain
set out westward from Franklin, Missouri. He planned
to trade with Indians around the Rockies. Once
he was there, though, Mexican troops urged him to go
down to Santa Fe. He sold his goods for good gain.
Next year he took wagons, followed the Cimarron,
avoided Raton Pass. Did that time after time.
Other traders joined in, settlers not far behind,
and soon ruts deep as ditches cut across the land.

In 1865 the US government
founded Fort Dodge to protect the trail from Cheyennes,
Kiowas, all the hostiles. Vast herds of buffalo
thundered upon plains hunters hunted far too hard.

In 1871 Henry Sitler built
a three-room sod ranch house five miles west of the fort.
Travelers stopped by. Some stayed. A general store
appeared, then a restaurant, blacksmith shop, dance hall,
saloon, and such. Profits were high. Front Street was born.

In 1872 the new Atchison,
Topeka and Santa Fe Railroad reached the town.
Buffalo hides by the thousands were stacked and shipped.
Lawlessness reigned. Train masters visited soiled doves.
Drifters, soldiers, and locals argued. Boot Hill grew.

In 1876, the buffalo gone,
Texans drove their longhorns in, and things got hog rank
once more. While Wyatt Earp and Bat Masterson tried
to keep the lid on, saloons and doves multiplied.
Twelve hundred people occupied what had become
the Wickedest City in the West. Guns were banned
north of the tracks. Cowboys and gamblers mixed it up.
Businesses changed their names to Alamo, Lone Star,
Texas this and that. Cold beer was served. Caviar.
The Long Branch even had a five-piece orchestra.
Bankers got rich. Lots of the violence was lies.

In 1882 the fort closed. Farmers plowed
grazing land to plant wheat. Boot Hill was history.

In 1886 the cattle drives were done.

In time ambitious citizens began to scheme;
to buy the legend told by nickelodeons
and dime novels and Western films and radio
and TV shows; to redo Front Street and Boot Hill,
places pilgrims from Poughkeepsie might pay to see.

Boot Hill

Above blank plains,
all that remains
of lives of crime:
graves without bones
and names on stones
ransomed from time.

Southwestern Kansas, 1897

Land a hundred miles west of Haviland.

A horizontal line, barely curved, cuts
the photograph in two; the lower half
is treeless earth; the upper, cloudless sky.

No railroad tracks. No barn. No horse. No cow.
No chickens. No picnic. No quilting bee.
No school. No dance. No prairie fire. No plague
of locusts. No dust storm. No drought. No hail.
No tornado. No cholera. No debt.
No Indians. Not even loneliness.

Only this: in the center, on that edge,
a tiny spot, rectangular, at first
maybe a blemish in the positive,
then the focus of dismay—someone's house.

Highway 56

Prancing at the edge
of a wheatfield: a ring-necked
pheasant, fanciest
thing you'll see en route between
Satanta and Santa Fe.

Panhandle Woman

I moved out here to find
something besides
cities. Well, look around.
I did—in spades.

Oklahoma

Hard hats nursing beers
lean on a pickup behind
a cinder-block bar,
night falling slow as the sweet
snarl of a steel guitar.

Alexandre Hogue, *Dust Bowl* (1933)

Low sun like a violent star
bursts above the violet air,
dusky glare burning on the bare
land turned to sand, a wind-torn war
zone of dry storms, broken barbed wire,
tracks across dunes going nowhere.

Dalhart, Texas

After a long day
on the road, forlorn
in a run-down room
at the Best Western,
I check the Yellow
Pages for somewhere
to dine. There's an ad
for Betty's Queen O'
Cream in Stratford that
counsels me to ask
for Lulu's Special—
eat in or take out.

A town away, but
what more do I need?

Uncle Bill's West Texas Ranch

Spread so big
he came home
by airplane
and then swam
naked in
a stock tank.

Lone Star

Borders on borders
in boundless orders,
from web to abyss,
from mirror to wall:

small problems for us,
nightmares for others,
mysteries of loss
and murder for all.

Prickly Pear

Skin's like Satan's, but
jelly made from the thing's fruit—
God's own condiment.

Fear and Loathing in the Grasslands

On a radio station
I tune in outside Clayton,
two cowmen have their say on
how your kids go bad if
you don't beat them enough,
how to control your wife,
how to ask God for rain,
how to grow lots of beef.

In Eastern New Mexico

When locals, after another day's load
of the same old hardscrabble scrounge,
gather at the Whiskey the Road
                              to Ruin Lounge,
happy hour, in keeping with the style
out here in Logan, lasts awhile.

In October 1541, Coronado Writes to the King of Spain about the Llano Estacado

I reached plains so vast
I could not see their limit
anywhere I went.
Though I journeyed over them
leagues on end, I found
no landmarks. It was as if
the ocean had swallowed me.

Tierra Encantada

Forsaken houses across the wide plains
gulfing Highway 54 story sad
tries at settling raw land: rubbles of stones
and shattered wood, wind-flayed, sun-pounded hulks,
dead dreams calcined under the hawk-haunted
sky. Out this way, Coronado's men, mad
and maundering, sought gold the Indians
never had. Fossils and dinosaur bones
abound up north—deep time's phantom jungles.
South lie featureless miles and miles and miles.
Further west stretch the Manzanos' foothills
and other sites otherwise enchanted.

Sixty in Springer

At the Fina station you fill
your tank unconsciously until
you notice, down the street,
Lombardy poplars, a whole wall
of changeful fall, fountains of tall
flames, colors bittersweet.

George McJunkin Discovers Folsom Man

One day, riding down
an arroyo, he remarks
the bones of some huge,
unusual animal,
then, later, finds fine flint points.

Jiggs Porter Remembers
Ranching during the 1930s

That was a horrible thing—the Dust Bowl.
You couldn't see a mile. And then it went
to raining. And then the government came
and shot the cows and calves. And then the rain
stopped. The grass died. But things weren't always bad.

In spring we'd brand at Crow Creek. Then we'd trail
up to the mountains and ship the herd out
at Colfax. Wintertime, well, wintertime
was different. At twenty below we chopped
ice for the cattle, rode plenty of fence
through snow. And we fed some. You had to do
what you had to do on those cold, short days.
Maybe we'd play some poker too or work
rawhide. I must have made a million quirts.

We ate a lot of turkey, deer, and elk.
I killed enough of those critters to dam
the Cimarron and the Vermejo both.
We operated on a shoestring. Sure,
I was tough on the crews, but I did try
to be fair. Nothing slipped. The chores got done.

There was a bucker called Payday I'd ride
for a fifteen-cent pack of Lucky Strikes.
When I think back on it, I realize
that's all I ever wanted out of life.

Eagle Nest

Mountain lake,
sky mirror,
remain calm

while I stop
for breakfast
by your shore.

Taos Pueblo

Early-morning sun as clear
as Rio Pueblo water, still
no other visitors. I walk
about, as if in a museum.
A woman stokes the fire
in an *horno*. Balmy scent
of piñon smoke. What
has changed in ten centuries?
Story on story: straw-and-mud
strata so long inhabited.

I kneel beside the stream
and lift a pebble out
of the cool flow down from
the Taos' sacred Blue Lake
high in the mountains. Not
to help memory but to fill
a hole in me, I pocket it.
Then sudden unease:
by this, if nothing else, I am
the thief of all that time.

A Photograph of Kit Carson

Here's the old scout the year
death struck: a solemn face
worn by pain and regret,
still filled with the wild's fear
(so many nights out there,
a blanket for a bed
away from the fire's glare,
a rifle by his side,
saddle a barricade),
where peace has yet no place.

The Art of R. C. Gorman

One
Indian
moment in
sunny sandstone
land again forms an
icon: round, warm woman.

Barbara Sachi's Photograph *Café with Auto with Café with Auto . . .*

In Chimayó, the day before
Palm Sunday, infinite regress
of this lowrider Cadillac
parked right in front of the same place
painted on its panels, there this
selfsame lowrider Cadillac
parked in precisely the same place
it's parked here and now, the same place
painted on *its* panels—way back,
down through the opiate abyss
in Chimayó, the day before
the day before the day before . . .

Early Spring in Española

Slightly brighter
light rises from
cruising lowriders'
slow chrome.

White Rock Overlook

When I arrive at the trailhead,
two huskies, almost alike, come
out of the blue, greet me. They go
along for the stroll to the edge
of the canyon. The river flows
far below. Immense air in all
that openness once carried off
ashes of a cousin I knew
so well he might have been my twin.
The dogs return with me and stop
at the trailhead. Each smiles goodbye.

Los Alamos

Because he has not found fame
through willful action,

Oppenheimer has a change
of heart and so, detached,

directs the play of others' plots,
politics of atoms;

reads *Bhagavad Gita*;
lives by Krishna's laws.

And somewhere far from here
people burn like neutron stars.

The Valle Grande Caldera

1
In the Frijoles Canyon ecotone
the Anasazi built their homes along
one high talus-heaped Swiss-cheese wall of tuff
and stayed hundreds of years—though they had left
that pink rock by the time the Spanish came.
Above the viga sockets: petroglyphs
opaque as constellations without names.

2
Barely a century after Lamy
watched as Italian masons closed his great
hollow of Romanesque anomaly
in the archdiocese of Santa Fe,
Archbishop Sanchez and his priests, accused
of sexual misconduct and abuse,
give holier-than-thou apologies.

3
The valley-torn Pajarito Plateau
fingers out from peaks behind which a hole
big as a county yawns. God knows, the bomb
fanatics at Los Alamos made some
craters, but this was formed ages before
we had equations to speak of such force.
It will outlive numbers' oblivion.

Tsankawi Sky

A pine ladder extends
far above broken adobe.
I whisper to myself:
Jack and the Beanstalk.

Ansel Adams

Your caring, rigorous eyes
floated above your smile
like that precise
                    moon
over Hernandez, New Mexico,
those luminous crosses and tombstones.

Trained to music, you played
the camera like a fine piano—
not guesswork but art, defined and controlled.

Learn, you said, to fix what is beheld:
isolate
form into abstraction, yet realize,
like Cézanne, what is felt.

You taught us the world
is made of light,
specific light;
is perishable.

Abiquiu

Clouds' black fluorescence
above blood-red hills: distance,
power, my absence.

Georgia O'Keeffe in New Mexico

By some spiritual accident
a train detour first took her there.

After she left, in thought she kept
returning. Then she did for real—

for empty canyons, sharp-edged light,
earth tones, silence, clean sky. She stayed

the rest of her oddball life, changed
all of it into oils, may still

wander piñon and juniper
beneath her Cerro Pedernal.

Pueblo Bonito

Dusk, time-kilned ruin,
dust, wind, tattered webs: even
the spiders have gone.

Highway 666

Not anymore.
That number's been
changed. Vandals kept
stealing the signs.

William A. Suys Jr., *Abbondanza I*

A painting offered among the fashionable
must-haves advertised in *Santa Fe Magazine*,
it depicts a smiling young woman who holds up
the skirt of her striped black-and-gold summery dress
like a basket overflowing with chiles, squash,
melons, grapes, tomatoes, and more, all pouring forth,
a cornucopia spilled out between full breasts,
with casual touches (short stems on roundnesses)
suggestive of her own nipples barely concealed
by narrow straps—the environs inchoate, dark,
maybe like land about a lost illegal's dreams.

B. B. Dunne

Here at La Fonda, on the wall:
a portrait of him dressed Chinese,
looking almost inscrutable.

Surely eccentric to a fault
even for the Santa Fe art
colony in its prime, he talked

a lot about chile that might
burn the enamel off your teeth
or—much the same—some beautiful

creature seen passing on the street.
Once had the front door of his house
carved in the shape of a life-size

Venus de Milo and then let
no woman come inside unless
her figure was a perfect fit.

At the Pink Adobe

Three nuns on the walk
by the Dragon Room Bar break
out in a cancan.

Bull-Roarer

Whirler.
Whizzer.
Hummer.

Buzzer.
Boomer.

Thunder.

July Rain in the Sangre de Cristos

Virgas: scumbled streaks,
gauze of ghost water never
getting to the ground.

The Staircase of the Loretto Chapel

The last day of the novena the sisters prayed
for a staircase to span the impossible space
from the floor to the choir loft, a carpenter came.
No one knew him. With only a hammer, a saw,
and a T square, he built this perfect piece of work —
a two-turn spiral way, reaching twenty feet high —
in six months. Then he vanished without recompense.
Some say he was Saint Joseph himself. Believe what
you will. The source of its wood is a mystery.
It has no central support. It contains no nails.

María Benítez at the Radisson

For her,
flamenco's art
is passion. When she slips
into the thrummed music and lets
go, she gives herself up
wholly to the moment. Her hips
sway on their own, her breasts held high, her back
erect, tense, muscled like a snake. The wooden floor,
a soundboard around her, echoes the quick
tapping of heels, clapping of hands, clacking of castanets
in cadence, layered scarlet satin of her dress aswirl
through the cabaret smoke as if she has turned all
flame. Then, at the very peak
                              of frenzy, her glance
takes you, makes something deep
in you shudder so you know what
corazón means and that this, once she comes
to a perfectly abrupt stop,
is how one does
its dance.

Mourning Doves

In the soft time before the sun
etches the Jemez Mountains, sound
those dulcet sad callings among
sage, juniper, cholla, and pine.

They tell of what I've left behind
and hint at what I'll take along
awhile. By now I understand
all Virgil's tears of things intend.

Santa Fe Dawn

Sun glances over
a Sangre de Cristo peak,
then, like a flare, stares.

October at Rancho Viejo

Wiping russet loess
off the windowsill—
whiff of nothingness
in the piny chill.

Tecolote

Frosty predawn
still, new snow thick
on Truchas Peak:

that low slow call
of the full moon
down in my skull.

Piñon

This tree whose delicious nut
conquistadors would commend
as unlike anything back
in Spain now suffers a bleak
death from the long, ancient drought
cycle—with bark beetles and
fungus to boot—that once brought
hunger sufficient to make
the Anasazi move out.

Cabezón Peak

To Sky's open mouth
Earth offers this ample breast.
Thus it longtime was
before Oñate arrived
with friars and matchlock guns.

Louis Owens at Albuquerque International, July 24, 2002

For him the sky's the limit—so we thought,
acclaiming what he was and what he taught,
but something missing stalled him, something not
shared, some Cherokee-Choctaw-Irish knot
of nought, that morning someone heard a shot
echoing from the airport parking lot.

Ben Wittick, *Tzashima and Her Husband, Governor of Laguna, Laguna Pueblo, ca. 1885*

Posed with the typical synthetic rocks,
they stare into optical emptiness.
He holds a bow in which he seems to have
no interest. She wears expectable
ornaments. Pots are arranged at their feet.

The backdrop, turreted Victorian
mansion and manicured grounds, doesn't quite
reach the photo's right edge, studio space
behind revealed, civilization's veil
too small to blanket such estranged deceit.

Ácoma Pueblo

A village aloft: all
soul-haunted wall on wall
of homes from times long by-
gone, lines guiding the eye
beyond—to row on row
of graves beset with small
crosses, far mountains, dry
plains that fan out below
immeasurable sky.

Matanza in Belén

No feedlots loom here
where men cleave and cook
meat in tank-like pots
in the open air
on the posse grounds
opposite Wal-Mart.

This is harvesting,
not hiding what's killed
in windowless plants,
plastic packages,
but dealing death straight
so people can eat
at long tables decked
to celebrate all
the lives going on.

And they won't fuss much
with the paradox.

The Very Large Array

In the bare desert air
this matrix of an ear
listens for life out where

forever empties. Year
by year there's nothing there
or nothing it can hear.

Trinity Site

Right here
earth got a sun that ghosted us with fear
and made our daft world dafter,
dividing time once more
between before
and after.

Chiaroscuro

In White Sands the mice
are white. In the Malpais,
just north, they are black.

Hillsboro

Southeast of the Black Range,
where gold and silver reigned
as kings, everything's once

upon a time. Lank skinks
scuttle through dreams of mines.
Nothing booms. Days drag on.

The owner of the clock
shop can't recall now how
long he's been living here.

Roswell

After you've heard enough
about the incident,
government cover-ups,
and all the rest, you pay
too much for some crushed ice
topped with fresh "alien juice,"
walk away, look for shade.

The Navajo Point of View

When a tree falls
in the bosque,
it's always heard.

Kingston

Once a silver boom town
of brothels and saloons
and seven thousand fools,
merchants, upstarts, and knaves,
it's still a place—although
the population's down
to thirty-two or so—
where dynamite is used
for digging hard-rock graves.

Lunch in Old Mesilla

Tank stocked with piranhas up front,
walls of black lava all about,
I sit in La Posta, drink beer,
eat beans and tamales, and muse
on those who dined here long before:
Carson, Pershing, Billy the Kid.

A History of New Mexico in Spanish

Luna.
Llano.
Lejano.
Llorona.

El Paso/Juárez

Once Elephant Butte Dam was built,
the Anglos would live well,
nestled in heaven's valleys. Still
do, indefinitely will—
as long as the smelters go at full tilt
south, in the barrios of hell.

Santo in an Abandoned House near Lordsburg

In this *nicho* like a small,
neglected chapel, old wall
crumbling to adobe scree:
a cracked wooden statuette,
polychrome paled, face drawn yet
still startled by sanctity.

Poco Tiempo

That can
wait. As
can that.

And that.

Sonoran Twilight

Blue haze of terpenes
floats above the chaparral:
the piñon's pale sigh.

Skeleton Canyon

There, where Geronimo, surrounded
among the lonely Peloncillos,
his last sanctuary, surrendered,
a jaguar pads through ocotillos.

Medicine Man

Geronimo, old coyote, colorful
trickster far wilier than any white

words, you're not history's suffering joke
in Oklahoma but ungraspable

spirit endlessly back in Mexico,
hidden in the mazy mountains of time,

and the fierce face you left in photos still
stirs remorse that scares hell out of us all.

Jeff Kidder (1875-1908)

He read dime novels by the ream
and practiced his fast draw
with whole cases of ammunition
till he was quicker
and slicker
than any man he knew. He saw
his one ambition
bloom like a waking dream:
he had indeed become
a real humdinger,
maybe the best gunslinger
in Arizona Territory.
As a ranger he fought,
more or less (when sober), on the side of the law.

But fate shortened his story.

The Mexicans caught up with him
in a whore's room
behind a cantina in Naco, Sonora. He got
gut-shot,
and in a house down the street there,
still young, handsome, hard-eyed,
and without fear,
he died.

Morgan S. Earp: A Short Short Story

Sometimes deputy marshal, he'd ridden shotgun for Wells Fargo on roads around Tombstone and even survived the shootout with the Clantons and McLaurys, only to find himself face down on a billiard table (ears still filled with the roar of the gunshot, glass everywhere, dark rain blowing in, Wyatt and others gathered about, hole through his middle, body numb), bleeding badly and wondering how a baby born in Pella, Iowa, had gotten into so much trouble.

Cilantro in Sonoita

Bite into a fat
fajita. Before

the taste of tortilla,
tomato, cheese,

chile, onion, beef:
a gust of summer

swirls, exorbitant,
into your nose.

Cochise County Realtor

Almost believing he's the bankrupt's friend,
he thinks it's been so easy to contrive
a deal to steal some gone-bust ranch out here.

But then he notices, parked in the drive,
a pickup full of cowboys full of beer
to help him understand how it will end.

Tucson

The Hohokam people built their homes here
a millennium past. The Santa Cruz
flowed then, did still when missionaries came
six centuries later and called the place
Stjukshon, "the spring at the black mountain's foot."

But now the river is gone. Only parched
arroyos remain, crisscrossed with the tracks
of collared lizards and teardrop-plumed quail
already scurrying under the rocks
and prickly pears as the Sonoran sun
rises toward midday and its heat death.

Bronze haze hangs above apartments, hotels,
motels, duplexes, condominiums.
The well-heeled breakfast by their swimming pools,
and four dozen golf courses get a douse
of off-peak water. Old Tucson prepares
for turkeys to gawk at Hollywood streets.
Fighters from Davis-Monthan slice the sky.

The Seri

Now few are left
of those who have
nothing but these

carvings to sell
and thus to save
a way of life.

Here is a fine
piece, a young seal,
polished to silk

softness, stone cool,
cut with smooth curves
in ironwood.

Finish is do.
The Seri know
no word for art.

Sabino Canyon in Spring

Along the winding trail grow
spiny ocotillo, plump
cacti of many types, pale
paloverde, flowers in bloom,
and saguaros with their armed
corrugations that swell out
or draw tight as they adjust
to seasonal rain or drought.

The object is to survive.
New life gets short shrift in soil
dry as bone meal where old roots
grow deep. Nature is not kind
in its beautifully correct
and grotesque economies.

North of Tucson: August

Dust devils at the feet
of the Santa Catalinas,
wildfires at their peaks.

Sabino Canyon in Fall

Balsa sticks, a stripped fan,
spread against sunk-sun rust:
saguaro skeleton,
water store long since passed.

Barrio Histórico

Suddenly clusters
of deep red along the street:
autumn's first *ristras*.

Edward Abbey's Grave

Somewhere in desert wilderness,
a mound of rocks beneath the vault
of Arizona blue, a place
(illegal, secret) with just this
for one who often sounded off
wrenchingly on such land's behalf:
his name and dates and epitaph—
"No Comment"—chiseled in basalt.

Arizona Borderland

Light candles, and let the souls
return. Fashion candy skulls.

Clean the crosses. Paint the stones.
Serve the *mole* and *pan*. Play

old songs. Make *retablos*. Pray.
Put fresh linen on the bed.

Sketch a comic skeleton.
Then live as much as you can.

When all has been said and done,
we're dreams and boxes of bones;

but on the Day of the Dead
life and afterlife are wed.

Old Route 66

All day long: hot sun
everywhere.
At night: cool neon
there and there.

Highway 40

This stretched main street
of fast food, fast
gas, fast almost
anything you'd
want runs across
the whole Southwest,
its emptiness
fast getting filled
with what hopes, gulled,
beguiled, beheld:
the Mother Road
for glutted need.

Las Vegas

As a flush takes
a straight,
here instinct breaks
restraint.

Margaritas at Lake Mead

Salt, triple sec, tequila, lime:
desert, sunset, sex, languor, time.

Nevada

As if from nowhere she came to the barn
a life ago, loosed her clothes in the dark,
lay soft on warm hay, and taught his young heart
reasons for madness. But in this far part
of the hard West some women can't stay. Dark
division empties their eyes; they depart
one sudden brittle morning with the stark
first light. They don't return. Who gives a darn?
An old man sipping bourbon in the dark
stares out his kitchen window at the barn.

The Great Basin

Think rock: ranges of tilted fault blocks rise
in mild slopes on one side, then at the top
drop, on the other, straight
down, down to ground continuing to pull apart.

Think green: bathtub rings on the foothills hint
how filled with life these valleys were
till heat held sway and glaciers waned
and evaporation began.

Think rain: the Sierra Nevada, shadowing
the desert, drinks most clouds dry before they arrive,
leaving barely sufficient wet
for sagebrush, silk grass, cactus, and creosote bush.

Think drainage: what water there is here flows
from a fifth of the West not to the sea
but inland to the termini
of lakes, marshes, salt flats, and sinks.

Think emptiness: a century ago
John Muir said this place was unredeemable
forever, and it still does not contain,
on average, two people per square mile.

Think solitude: roads seem to stretch
to nowhere and generally do,
and even the few cities grow, as if nothing would end,
with folks who don't know who they are.

Think myth: homesteads long left
to the sun's cooking, once
inhabited by bold buckaroo dreams of freedom, haunt
tired hearts like cattle skulls.

John Wesley Powell

Expedition boats beached
deep in the canyon, he ignores
his crew's mutinous plaints.
The Colorado rushes by,
dangerous, red.

He scribbles on.
This man who lost an arm
at Shiloh applies himself to nature—untamed,
sublime, like a woman. He can't
get close enough.

Grand Canyon

For the water, it was a path.
For the Anasazi and then
the Havasupai, it was home.
For the conquistadors, it was
an obstacle. For scientists,
it was something to be explored.
For artists, it was rock to paint
or photograph. For children, bored,
playing around the junipers,
it's an irrelevance. For all
the rest of us, tourists awestruck
along the brink of gaping space,
it's sculpted spectacle. We cluster
like flies on the lip of a wound.

A Ponderosa Pine in the Kaibab National Forest

Hug that huge old tree,
cheek up close to the red bark:
smell of vanilla.

Mountain Meadows, 1999

Years later Twain wrote that the whole United States
rang with the horrors of what hereabout occurred:
hapless pioneers hoodwinked, their bodies interred
posthaste after the bloodbath. Vengeance of the Lord
never came for wronged bones a backhoe excavates
by chance but Mormon guilt still purposely forgets.

Monument Valley

Water-carved, honed
by sand, frost-chilled,
sun-brazed, time-gnarled:

John Ford's background,
Navajos' world
of holy wind.

Native Poetry: The Lesson
of Canyon de Chelly

Song strung with story,
forces in counterpoint:
words
      from your heart
up,
   silences
from your head down.

Mesa Verde

So many once lived in these rooms of rock
hewn by hand and mortared with mud, floors stacked
in alcoves and caves along the cliff walls.

For all their lasting architectural
genius and sense of space, they, like us,
didn't stop building till they'd built too much.

Red Mountain Pass

Driving the Million Dollar Highway
winding south out of Ouray,
the edge
without railing or shoulder,
even a ridge
tread might engage,
you must
ignore the gorgeous gorge,
thousand-foot river cleft,
dappled with morning mist
that's just
a yard or so away
and trust
skill and instinct and not imagine
a problem with the engine
or brakes and not consider
the margin
of error, odds for or against
getting through, and not speak
of sheer
evacuating fear
until a massive peak
looms red
up to the left
and you're not dead.

A Bad Moment in Colorado

We were holding this here
reburial of exhumed
victims of the cannibal
Alferd, what's his name,
Packer (all that hell
happened a long time
back but still bothers some),
and the preacher said
(well I'll never, I'm sure,
forget what he said—
I guess he just had
to remind everyone,
as if the scene wasn't odd
enough) man does not
live by bread alone.

Pagosa Springs

Things have been going yuppie fine
on automatic pilot till
late one night outside an upscale
bar in a new strip mall, dizzy
from drinking way too much whiskey
(though I can't quite remember why),
weaving toward my SUV,
I feel that deep-down-death lonesome
sorrow about now what the hell
am I doing with my life, then,
stunned under the star-crystalled sky
spinning in a transparent skull,
I'm certain not many questions
are worth asking, but one of them
is this: Is there still a grizzly
living in the San Juan Mountains?

William H. Jackson Observes the Mount of the Holy Cross from the Summit of Notch Mountain

Jackson clambers over a mass
of jagged rocks, his gear at last
hauled to the top. He sees the cross
of snow and knows that all the grief
was worth it—for a photograph
proving God's country is out west
and Manifest Destiny blessed.

The Saga of Mart Duggan

Several years after this
feisty Irishman killed
Louis Lamb in Leadville,
his troubled life ended.

Soused and quarrelsome
after a late poker game,
he was sniped from behind
outside the Texas House.

Though theories abound
as to who did the deed—
he had his enemies—
the shooter's unknown still.

The town had become less
tense by then (thanks to him,
according to his fans),
but Lamb's widow danced,

as she'd vowed, on the boards
of the sidewalk stained
by his blood—and handed
his grieving wife her weeds.

Everett Ruess

After the wild within became the wild
without a guide, he pilgrimed on his own,
his need beyond what cities could impound.
At twenty he disappeared, an unknown
artist lusting for desert distances,
an adolescent looking for himself
in Utah's traplight void, a vagabond
for beauty. He'd crossed some beckoning threshold,
entered a world horizonless and lost and cold.

All the trackers found in the fractal twists
of Davis Gulch's cliffy narrow canyon
was two abandoned burros penned behind
a brush fence, marks where a bedroll had lain,
candy wrappers and such, empty condensed-
milk cans, random trail of back-and-forth prints
of boots, an enigmatic petroglyph
scratched in sandstone at the base of a door
in ancient ruins: NEMO 1934.

A Veteran Downwinder Talks about Snow Canyon

Back in the fifties, that was the wrong part
of Utah to make a flick in. John Wayne
played Genghis Khan. Great casting. A thing called
The Conqueror. The government assured
Dick Powell the place was safe from fallout
that blew east from the Nevada Test Site
over by Yucca Lake. Later a lot
of the cast and crew died of cancer. Guess
none of them conquered very much. But now
it's all been fixed up into a state park.
Beautiful. Breathtaking. People camp out
there, thousands each year, since the government
assures us it's safe. Well, that's pure bullshit.
Death lies hidden and waiting in those dunes.
Half-life of some of that poisonous stuff
is near the half-life of eternity.

The Southwestern Grid

Like *Yé'ii* in Navajo sand
paintings, hands holding nature's powers,
these latticework transmission towers,
long-waisted gods, straddle the land.

Teller House, Central City

The poor bastard she'd jilted drank
and drank before he chalked
her portrait on the barroom floor
and then abruptly died:

a face that would indeed have bought
the soul of any man,
those faithless burning eyes now cast
evermore to the side.

At William Cody's Grave

Come that final January
of his theatric soul,
even this legendary
hero's curtain would fall,
marking the ordinary
end of an epic role,
his whole show mortuary,
west of everything's call.

Country Love: Eastern Colorado

Imprisoned in cold, they spent
the gray spaces of dull days
listening to the clock's tick,
staring across the snow's glaze.

Nights they slept by fits and starts,
lay by turns insomnolent
with mute griefs and fears, agaze
at the stars' clouded descent.

God only knows how they went
on enduring such malaise,
but even February's thick
boredom couldn't freeze their hearts.

Garden of the Gods

I walk the wild
quiet and gather
myself together
until the hold
of the world's hum
begins to end.

Then slowly I'm
a lost and found
and feral child—
and headed home.

For Alain Lasfargues: An Epilogue

September eleventh was nearly three years past.
In Dodge City the country still felt deadly strange—
flags aloft, Jesus talk, militant attitudes.

We sat sipping wine by the chuck wagon, wan light
filtering through smoke that smelled of grilled meat.

After hours of interviewing, we had enough
raw footage. Later on, your art could fashion it
to show Europe the mythos of America.

Tired reenactors, stuck in character, lined up
for supper—Indians, mountain men, saloon girls,
gunslingers, cowboys—while we spoke in French
of why culling the truth is tricky, difficult.

The poet, you averred, quoting Cocteau,
consoles himself with the illusion that his work
is based on some more concrete mystery.
You told me the film would air on election day.

We laughed, and then we drank the bottle to the lees.

Acknowledgments

This project, supported by a sabbatical leave from the University of Kansas, began as a short in-progress collection titled "Southwestern Afflatus: Poems for a Land of Little Rain," which received the Frederick Manfred Prize from the Western Literature Association, an honor that wonderfully encouraged me to continue writing poetry about the American Southwest. Most of the poems included here derive from my own experiences. A few derive from anecdotes or information in the public domain. And a few are indebted to the following sources for specifics helpful to their composition:

Christensen, Jon. "The Great Basin: America's Wasteland Seeks a New Identity." *High Country News*, 3 April 1995, pp. 1, 8-9.

DeArment, Robert K., ed. *Deadly Dozen: Twelve Forgotten Gunfighters of the Old West.* Norman: University of Oklahoma Press, 2003.

Frantz, Laurie Evans. "Lake Valley Back Country Byway." *New Mexico Magazine*, December 2004, pp. 64-65.

Goetzmann, William H. *Exploration and Empire: The Explorer and the Scientist in the Winning of the American West* (1966; reprint ed., Austin: Texas State Historical Association, 1993).

Krakauer, Jon. *Into the Wild.* New York: Villard, 1996.

Niederman, Sharon. "Jiggs Porter: Ranching Maverick of Colfax County." *New Mexico Magazine*, September 2002, pp. 16-17.

O'Grady, John P. *Pilgrims to the Wild: Everett Ruess, Henry David Thoreau, John Muir, Clarence King, Mary Austin.* Salt Lake City: University of Utah Press, 1993.

Some of the poems in this collection, a few slightly revised, first appeared in the following publications, from which they are, with gratitude, reprinted: *Aura: Literary Arts Review, Coal City Review, Ecphrases: Poems as Interpretations of the Other Arts* (Topeka, KS: Woodley Press, 1989), *Ekphrasis: A Poetry Journal, From Hell to Jackson Hole: A Poetic History of the American West* (Rancho Murieta, CA: Bridge House Books, 2001), *Ilya's Honey, International Poetry Review, Into the Teeth of the Wind, I-70 Review, Lawrence Journal-World, Midwest Quarterly, Owen Wister Review, The Raintown Review: A Journal of Metrical Poetry, Southwestern American Literature, The Unicorn Captured* (Lawrence, KS: Cottonwood Review Press, 1980), *Underground Rag Mag, Violence and Grace: Poems about the American West* (Lawrence, KS: Cottonwood Press, 1993), *Wavelength: A Magazine of Poetry in Prose and Verse,* and *Westview.*

Finally, I owe much thanks to Gary Lechliter for his editing of this book and to the capable people in the College of Liberal Arts and Sciences Digital Media Services at the University of Kansas for making attractive text out of my Keatsian messes.

Michael L. Johnson, a Spur Award-winning writer, is the author of numerous poems, essays, and books concerning the American West, most notably *Violence and Grace: Poems about the American West*, *New Westers: The West in Contemporary American Culture*, *From Hell to Jackson Hole: A Poetic History of the American West*, and *Hunger for the Wild: America's Obsession with the Untamed West*.

www.ingramcontent.com/pod-product-compliance
Lightning Source LLC
Chambersburg PA
CBHW020915090426
42736CB00008B/640